D1565586

# LEADING
## FROM THE
# *Feminine*

A Guide to Accessing
Your Deeper, Feminine
Wisdom Needed
to Heal Our Global
Disconnection

LAURIE BENSON

Leading from the Feminine © 2022 Laurie Benson

Print ISBN: 978-1-66785-653-7
eBook ISBN: 978-1-66784-688-0

My work has evolved as my awareness has expanded.

From my beginnings in climate change, to founding an organization supporting women in agriculture, to where I sit today at the intersection of embodiment, trust, and deep knowing.

I have dedicated my life to opening doors of reconnection with ourselves, each other, and all living beings. The question, "What story, or deep wisdom, is living inside of you ready to be shared?" guides my work.

I am deeply passionate about today's opportunity to break down existing paradigms and borders and learn to move through the world guided by our deeper heart wisdom and the truth of our interconnection.

Laurie Benson
Buena Vista, Colorado USA
Traditional land of the Ute
inwardboundwomen.com

# Prologue

This book is a journey, not a sprint. You are meant to slowly move through the teachings and invitations, allowing them to land in your body in a way that brings true change. It will take time and patience, and be worth every ounce of energy you invest.

Change is the greatest gift in front of us right now. Change from what no longer serves, change from feeling unsure of our true power and voice, change from the old way of moving through the world.

I have broken this book into three sections. I recommend sitting with and revisiting the tools and resources in this section for as long as you need, until it truly feels at home in your body.

This isn't meant to be a book that you read in one or two sittings and then stick on a shelf. Its offerings expand as your awareness deepens. It is a guide, an invitation, tried activities and practices, that have changed and transformed the journey and trajectory for many.

This is your opportunity to make a commitment to yourself. To know that you are worth it, and that this commitment is not only for you, but also your family, community, and all of life.

We are standing at a critical moment in the evolution of humanity. What we do right now will impact how, and if, we all move forward together.

Someone once shared with me that they move through life holding this question, "Am I being a good ancestor?"

That sharing had a profound impact on me, and I also hold it close. So now I will ask you, as you step into this time of possibility, dive into lessons, activities, and opportunities that allow you to connect with the deep, interconnected wisdom of your heart, "Are you being a good ancestor?"

I believe the answer is absolutely, yes. It is why you are here reading these words. You care. You care about yourself and the way you interact with the world. You care about our collective future. You are interested in tearing down the current paradigms and stepping into a new way for the generations yet to come.

So am I, and I'm grateful and honored to be on this journey with you.

"What does it mean to reclaim the feminine?

It means to honor our sacred connection to
life that is present in every moment."

~ Llewellyn Vaughan-Lee

# Section 1: Laying the Ground Work

## Reclaiming Balance

It isn't an accident that we are here, on earth, at this point in time. We are here because there is great work to be done. A fact that can feel overwhelming at best.

Daily, we see and hear about the dysfunction and destruction of communities, governments, the planet, and so much more. The questions, "What *can* I do? What *do* I do?", can shut us down and leave us moving through our days in ways that feel less and less connected, less and less our true selves.

The beautiful side of this global story is that the work we can do begins with us right here, right now. By turning inward and finding our true center and inner wisdom, we hold the power to create incredible change - change that comes from feminine wisdom and consciousness. Change that allows all beings to move forward in a way that is more centered, more focused on connection and unity.

This work is for everyone, regardless of gender. The voice of the feminine has been silenced for thousands of years, and our greatest work is reclaiming that balance within us all. But don't be mistaken, although the work requires us all, it begins with the women. It begins with us remembering what it means to lead from the feminine.

The change needed entails remembering the voice of our intuition verses the voice of fear, ego, and learned responses. Remembering what it feels like and looks like when we allow ourselves to pause, and create space for the larger work and actions that are waiting to emerge. We pause, instead of pushing forward in the same ways that have led to the world we are experiencing today.

Our work is simple, but not easy. We have this knowledge deep within us, but it's been hidden for many generations.

We have the honor and privilege of listening and remembering for ourselves, the generations yet to come, and the generations that have already passed. We have the opportunity to do things differently and watch the ripple effect that comes when we focus on our powerful and incredibly important feminine qualities and values - our deep feminine wisdom.

The path of the feminine is the path of connection and healing that the world so desperately needs.

> "Understanding the wisdom and transformative nature of the feminine is essential if we are to move individually and collectively out of the wasteland created by the masculine consciousness and values, if we are to awaken to a deeper and more natural awareness of our own nature as well as that of all life, if we are to re-attune our soul with the soul of the world. The feminine can give us the tools we need to begin the work of both the individual and global transformation."
>
> ~ Llewellyn Vaughan-Lee

## We Begin

*I recommend you have a journal with you as you move through this book. There are many prompts and questions to facilitate the lessons presented. The questions in bold are meant to be answered, so take your time and enjoy where this process takes you in your own personal exploration.*

Let's jump right in with some of the beautiful words that represent feminine leadership. (See the list on the next page.)

As you read through the following list, let these words land in your body and see which ones resonate with you.

We will come back and visit this list several times as we move through this work together.

Go through the words and identify: what you currently embody, what you would like to embody, and what doesn't resonate with you.

Notice what on the list surprises you and what additional qualities you would like to add.

I recommend using colored highlighters to mark the different words and the categories they fall under for you.

# Feminine Leadership Qualities and Values:

Key: Orange = I embody / Pink = I want to embody / Yellow = Doesn't resonate

Activism
Adaptability
Allowing
Authenticity
Awareness
Balance
Beauty
Belonging
Caring
Centered
Change
Co-creation
Collaboration
Community
Compassion
Connection
Contentment
Contribution
Confidence
Cooperation
Courage
Creativity
Culture
Curiosity
Dignity
Discovery
Diversity
Embodiment
Environment
Equality
Ethics
Faith
Family
Feminine
Forgiveness
Freedom
Friendship
Fun
Future Generations

Generosity
Global
Grace
Gratitude
Growth
Harmony
Health
Home
Honesty
Hope
Humility
Humor
Inclusive
Instinctual
Integrity
Inter-connection
Intuition
Joy
Justice
Kindness
Knowledge
Leadership
Learning
Listening
Love
Making a Difference
Magic
Nature
Nurture
Openness
Optimism
Parenting
Patience
Peace
Principaled
Personal Fulfillment
Receptive
Reliability
Resourcefulness

Respect
Responsibility
Sacred
Safety
Security
Self-Expression
Self-Respect
Serenity
Service
Simplicity
Softness
Spirit
Spirituality
Stewardship
Success
Teamwork
Time
Together
Tradition
Travel
Trust
Truth
Understanding
Uniqueness
Unity
Usefulness
Vision
Vulnerability
Well-being
Wholeheartedness
Wholeness
Wisdom

Write Your Own:

## Indigenous Wisdom
## The Prophecy of the Eagle and the Condor

In December 2012, my family and I spent time with Indigenous Peoples from Costa Rica, Nicaragua, United States, Ecuador, Guatemala, and Mexico.

It was during this gathering that I first learned of the Prophecy of the Eagle and the Condor. The Prophecy speaks of the potential for humanity to enter a new level of consciousness. It is now up to us to act on this wisdom, and ensure this new consciousness is allowed to emerge. It is up to us to help the Condor rise.

*The Eagle and the Condor is an ancient prophecy that speaks of human societies splitting into two paths - that of the Eagle, and that of the Condor. The path of the Condor is the path of the heart, of intuition, and of the feminine. The path of the Eagle is the path of the mind, of the industrial, and of the masculine.*

*The prophecy shares that the Eagle and Condor used to fly together in harmony and balance and in the 1490s, we would begin a 500-year period during which the Eagle people would become so powerful that they would virtually drive the Condor people out of existence. The prophecy says that during the following 500-year period, beginning in 1990, the potential would arise for the Eagle and the Condor to come together again, fly in the same sky, and create a new level of consciousness for humanity.*

This isn't a prophecy about men and women. We all hold the masculine and feminine within ourselves. The balance we are striving for takes place within us all, as well as within the structures we currently operate under.

I think it's important to share that while it feels like we are at the extreme points of this prophecy, at the point of near extinction, I believe the opposite is actually true. I believe that everything we are experiencing today is because we are almost at the point of reconnection and balance where the Eagle and the Condor again fly together in harmony, and a new level of consciousness is ushered in.

Those comfortable in the Eagle paradigm are frightened by the unknown of this "new" state of balance, and are pushing back with all of their might. We are seeing this fear and push back play out as war, racism, greed, and so much more.

The opportunity and the work in front of us is great. It is the time of the Condor Rising.

Whether you know it or not, you have just committed to returning the world to a place of balance by stepping into this work. You are the change the world needs. Let's join together and create the incredible push needed to tip the scales back into a place of balance and unity.

## The Time of the Feminine
## Mayan Prophecy 2012

On December 21, 2012, the Mayan Long Count Calendar came to an end. Many saw this ending as a sign of our demise. There were doomsday theories and apocalyptic warnings that our world would soon be over. And it was, just not in the way they feared.

"An Apocalypse (Greek: "lifting the veil" or "revelation") is a disclosure of something hidden from the majority of mankind in an era dominated by false hook and misconception, i.e., the veil to be lifted."

~ Wikipedia

By stepping into this work of connecting with and honoring your feminine wisdom, you are lifting the veil. The veil of the old paradigms that no longer serve humanity or the planet. The Mayans were correct that there would be an ending, it is up to us to honor and welcome the new beginning.

> "Both the Hopis and the Mayans recognize that we are approaching the end of a World Age...In both cases, however, the Hopi and Mayan elders do not prophesy that everything will come to an end. Rather, this is a time of transformation from one World Age into another.
>
> The message they give concerns our making a choice of how we enter the future ahead. Our moving through with either resistance or acceptance will determine whether the transition will happen with cataclysmic changes or gradual peace and tranquility.

The same theme can be found reflected in prophecies of many other Native American visionaries from Black Elk to Sun Bear."

~Joseph Robert Jochmans

## Why Are These Prophecies So Important?

The power and gifts of these prophecies from around the world come in many forms.

I believe one of their greatest gifts is providing the awareness that there are people still with us today who knew that humanity would reach this point of environmental, economic, and humanitarian collapse.

They knew that we would see extreme climate fluctuations, an increase in war and oppression, economic failure, and much more. And these people, who carry this knowledge and wisdom, are some of the kindest and happiest people I've ever spent time with.

Along with these grim predictions, they know and see the opportunity. The opportunity that lies within our reconnection with the divine feminine, our collective heart wisdom, which is the doorway to our interconnection.

So this is where our work begins. And it truly will be the most important work of our time. This transformation and heightened awareness has to happen one person at a time. It truly begins with you, right here, right now.

We have to understand what this shift looks like and feels like for each of us individually, as well as on a global level.

The collective power of this knowledge will bring about the necessary change. The incredible power of our feminine wisdom, the divine feminine, is waiting for our remembering.

Together, we will understand where our power lies within this wisdom, and how it changes the way we move through the world.

We will recognize that the work we continue to do for ourselves has a ripple effect greater than we can even imagine. We begin the work, looking inward, and then acquire the tools and awareness necessary to put our learnings and insight into play.

This deep inner work translates into action when we  move through the world in a new way - interacting and witnessing from that place of feminine consciousness and true connection.

We haven't ever been here before. Prophecies have brought us to this point. Indigenous People around the globe knew we would end up where we are today, and now we all step into the unknown together. This is a time of breaking through old paradigms, redefining and restructuring all that we believed to be important and true.

This is the time of the feminine consciousness, the Condor Rising, and we are the ones being called front and center in this work.

Now is the time for deep feminine wisdom to come together with the masculine consciousness to create a new understanding of life and wholeness. It is time for the Eagle and the Condor to again fly together in harmony. A time of new understanding that is necessary to heal the world.

## How Will This Impact Your Life?

Without assuming to know where you currently are on your journey, I'll share some of the points of entry for various women I've worked with over the years.

*"I feel like everything is stuck, or stagnant. No matter what I try, things won't take hold."*

*"I can't imagine how to turn what I love into work. It would never make money and support me."*

*"I have this dream of what I would love to be doing, and then, I have a long list of all the reasons it won't work."*

*"The world feels so broken that some days, I don't even want to get out of bed."*

*"I cannot even begin to identify with so many people in my family right now, let alone sit down at a dinner table with them."*

This work is a powerful invitation and tool to move through the world in a new way. You will no longer experience things as happening *to* you, but instead understand the roles you have been playing in your relationships and experiences, and step onto a powerful new path.

You are the only one who can step in and make this commitment to yourself. You will uncover powerful truths about yourself and your relationships. Your life will open up in incredible ways.

*And* you will create a ripple effect that reaches far and wide, opening the doors to global change. This isn't just about you, or me; it's about our opportunity, and ability, to shift the collective consciousness.

Sounds extreme, I know, but this is the power of leading from the feminine. By stepping into this work, you are returning to the place of balance that allows all of life to thrive and prosper.

## Why is this work important to you?

I invite you to take some time and make a list of all the reasons you are stepping in and saying yes to this journey.

**Why are you here doing this work?**

**What feels stuck?**

**What are you hoping to accomplish?**

**What are you hoping to let go of and change?**

**What are your greatest dreams?**

**What are your hopes and wishes for the world?**

You get the idea. Don't hold back; make your list as big as you can. (We will return to this list through out this book and our work together.)

## Our Presence Is Needed
## Presence Within Ourselves and In the Current Moment

> "The world needs the presence of women
> who are awake to their spiritual light, and
> who can work with the substance of life
> in order to heal and transform it."
>
> ~Llewellyn Vaughan-Lee

This work may not resonate with everyone. I don't believe that there is one magic way for all of us to access the feminine and reach a new level of awareness that allows us to move differently through the world.

There are many entry points that will hopefully bring us all to this place of allowing, embodiment, and connection.

This work and sharing is based on my training, education, experiences, interpretations, intuition, wonderful mentors and guides, and deeper knowing.

**Let's Begin!**

# Section 2: Part 1: The Work

I invite you to slow down and take your time in this section. The work we will move through requires patience and commitment.

Remember what you are here to accomplish, let go of, and step into.

You are creating new habits, beginning a new conversation with your body, re-learning how to listen to your heart and its powerful guidance.

This work is a deep, embodied awakening. Look back at the list you made of why you are here and what you want from this work. This section will offer tools to assist you in finding the answers and guidance to these questions and desires.

So slow down and come back to these practices and inquiries daily for a week, several weeks, months, however long it takes, to make them common practice. You want them to become second nature as your move through your day.

You have shown up for this work because you are ready. Don't doubt or second guess your decision to be here. This is where you jump in with both feet and enjoy the ride!

## Somatic Awareness Work

Our work together begins with a deeper understanding of where you experience things within your body. Where do you feel sadness? Which part of your body do you exist within when you are stuck in your old stories and patterns? How does this hold you back? Where do you feel joy and freedom, and how do you come back to this place within your body when you need to?

To find these answers, you begin by allowing yourself time to pause. There is great power in pausing, and this tool is accessible to you at all times.

**Let's move through a somatic awareness exercise**:

I invite you to close your eyes, take a deep breath, and just pause. Notice your breath, and then, put your attention on the exhale.

With your next exhale, take the opportunity to relax into your entire body.

From this relaxed state, remember something that made you upset recently, someone who stole your power. Maybe it was something or someone at work, maybe at home. Sit with that memory for a moment, and then, notice where you are feeling it within your body. Do you feel it in your chest, neck, stomach? Just notice without judgement or stories.

And once you've identified where you feel it, see if you can come up with a few words that describe this feeling - heavy, dark, sticky, tight.

**Where do you feel this experience?**

**What words describe this feeling?**

**Write down any additional awareness and thoughts.**

Now come back to your breath. Using the exhale as an opportunity to release, let go of that memory.

When you've returned to a more relaxed state, I'd like you to think of something that made you happy. Maybe it was dinner with friends or family, watching a sunset, going on vacation. And then place yourself back in that time and place. Remember any sounds, smells, what did you see?

Once you are solidly back in this memory, bring your attention again to your body. Where are you feeling this experience? When you've identified this energy within yourself, come up with a few words to describe it - light, fluttery, calming, exciting.

**Where do you feel this experience?**

**What words describe this feeling?**

**Write down any additional awareness and thoughts.**

(This exercise is one point of entry for the work we will do moving forward. When you understand where you are experiencing things in your body, and the filters you experience them through, your awareness expands significantly. This is the ground work for stepping into your true self and bringing your dreams to life. That doesn't mean you stop here if you can't feel either memory, it means your work right now is around building that awareness as you move forward.)

This exercise can be tough, and can create the first real road block, or the temptation to stop. Don't! Everything worth while takes time and effort. The benefits of this embodied awareness are life changing. Most of us know where we experience (feel) the negative in our bodies, the positive can be more challenging. So, as you move through your day and find yourself smiling, laughing, happy, pause and do a quick check-in. Where are you feeling that joy? No judgement, just awareness, and then move on.

The more you tune into your body, the more it will respond to your inquiries. You are creating a new relationship and conversation that is worth every ounce of energy you invest.

Tara Brach; a psychologist, meditation guide, author, and teacher, offers incredible work and support for becoming further aware of what you are feeling and experiencing. What it feels like to "come home to our bodies." (More information can be found in the 'Resources Section' at the end of the book.)

## The Power of the Pause

Pausing and centering.

The pause is the allowing. You don't need to immediately react or have an answer to everything in front of you. The greater invitation is to pause, feel, and intuitively listen before you engage. This moment of inquiry can completely shift outcomes and our ability to move through the world in alignment with our greater truths and heart-wisdom.

Think about a recent situation where you walked away unsettled because you didn't feel heard, couldn't find the words, or said something you didn't mean.

When you ignore the invitation to pause, and instead, push through from that place of tension and anxiety, you miss incredible opportunities. You can't see yourself clearly, nor can others see the true you because you are engaging, and communicating through your old stories and experiences.

Let's practice right now. What do you have coming up in your day that might challenge you to be your best self?

Think about some of the qualities of feminine leadership from the list at the beginning of the book - allowing, intuition, centered power, whichever ones resonated with you, and take a deep breath.

Feel these qualities move through you with that breath. Notice how it feels to truly embody them in this moment. Now on the exhale, let go of any feelings of tension and worry.

From this centered, feminine space, think about the following questions:

**Where are you existing in your body when you think about this situation?** (If you aren't sure, move back through the somatic awareness exercise, again and again, until you begin to feel where the energy is living.)

**Is this space aligned with the feminine qualities you want to express?** (Remember your list and your additions.)

**If yes, do you understand the place in your body you should be occupying when you enter into this situation?**

**Does this bring a sense of freedom?**

**If no, what can you do to move into that centered space before you engage in the upcoming situation?**

**Can you give yourself some time before you need to interact, time to know you are engaging from that place of joy and freedom?**

The only thing that changes in these situations is you. That's all you can control.

I want to put those last two sentences on repeat because they offer so much freedom. We are only responsible for ourselves. We can stop trying to change the behavior of others, and feel the immense release that comes when we stop shifting our reactions and responses according to the needs and wants of everything and everyone around us.

Your ability to pause, center, and then show up as the best possible version of yourself is freeing for you, and for those you are interacting with. It allows you to go to bed at night knowing you truly did your best. It allows others to see and hear who you truly are, allows your gifts and incredible power to shine.

What more could you truly want than to show up in your centered power and pure love, and stop being controlled by the actions and reactions of others?

This ability is world changing. This new perspective dissolves barriers and allows you to see the possibilities and opportunities in conversations and interactions that aren't clear when you engage from your old stories, beliefs, and learned behavior.

Pausing and centering truly shifts paradigms. Know that when you open yourself to this change, you do it not only for yourself, but for greater human unity as well.

Remember that you are stepping into this work to create a new path forward.

This new skill and awareness doesn't mean that everything will go your way, or that every interaction will end harmoniously. What changes is your interaction *with* and reaction *to* these experiences. When you understand where you are feelings things, you open the door to a powerful level of engagement and freedom.

When you pause, and move through interactions from this place of freedom and joy within your body, you truly know at the end of the day that you showed up as the best possible version of yourself.

Things no longer happen *to* you. Instead, you show up as a witness and student, becoming aware of the stories moving through others, and how their comments and reactions are truly just reflections of where they are on their own personal journey.

I can now viscerally feel when someone is sharing through their pain or joy. This insight allows me to witness the interaction in a completely new way.

I understand that what they are sharing is being processed through filters within their own body and impacting the way they communicate and experience the world. It opens the door to a new level of empathy, engagement, and freedom.

Emotions created by your interactions and experiences flow through you instead of getting stuck within you.

## Kind Curiosity

As you move through all of these exercises, during our time together and beyond, I want to stress kind curiosity.

Many of us have spent a long time perfecting the art of not feeling our emotions and experiences. We've learned to push through our days, in order to accomplish what we need to do, and keep moving forward.

All of the work we are doing, and will do, is simply creating a new layer of awareness. We are creating new habits which take time and commitment. If you don't feel one, or both, of the somatic awareness exercises within your body, that is okay, and you are absolutely not alone. Give these practices the gentle time and space they need to come to life for you.

The work now is checking in again and again until you start to feel something stirring. Also, recognize that with every pause and check in, you are creating change and accessing deeper wisdom within yourself. You are sending messages to your body that you are open to its wisdom and ready to feel what is being shared.

You are creating a new level of awareness that is going to completely shift your ability to step into your dreams and aspirations, change your relationships for the better, and change the way you see and value yourself. This new level of awareness is the door to finding the answers you are seeking, and your path forward.

Everything you need to know already lives within you. You are in the process of tapping into your powerful inner wisdom. It's life changing, and absolutely worth your commitment and work.

You are working toward freedom. Give yourself time. Give yourself space. Be kind to yourself in the process. You are worth the effort and deserve the incredible rewards waiting for you.

# Section 2: Part 2: The Deeper Work

This next phase of work becomes easier when you are aware of where you are feeling things in your body. If that is still elusive to you, please keep going back to the previous somatic awareness exercises. It can take time and commitment to reconnect with yourself in this way.

*This also feels like a good time to share that I host an online community for women where we support one another in this work. If you are feeling stuck, you truly aren't alone. We would love to have you join us at inwardboundcommunity.com.*

## Using Your Body as a Gauge

You can use this new awareness of what you are feeling within your body to gauge and filter your own thoughts, as well as the comments and actions of others.

Your body becomes a powerful ally in identifying whether comments and experiences are yours to hold and learn from, or should be let go of.

When you find yourself in triggering situations, pause and check in with your body. Recognize if you are in that space of tension, or that space of freedom and joy, and then, ask yourself these questions:

**Does this comment or interaction feel true to me? Is it mine to hold?**

**If so, what is it here to teach me?**

**If not, can I let it move right through me and not let it grab hold? Can I recognize that it is probably isn't my story?**

**What is my body telling me?**

## The Deeper Work

From this point forward, until you've created a habit of turning inward, I invite you to pause and check in twenty times a day. Just a quick pause, deep breath, tune into your body, notice, and move on.

Use cues during your day to create the opportunities to check in. Are you happy? *Check in.* Are you angry? *Check in.* Is there a beautiful sunset? *Check in.* Are you stuck in traffic? *Check in.*

What are you feeling? If you feel something, make a mental note, and move along. If you feel nothing, don't turn that into a story; again, notice with kind curiosity and move along.

Through pausing and turning inward, you are creating a new level of self-awareness, a new conversation with your body. You are shining a light into your shadow and breaking down the darkness that's been hiding there for, most likely, quite a while.

## Shadow Self

*Throughout this book, I share the highlights and overviews of the different areas of study, and the teachers, that have deeply influenced my journey. More information about these ideas and thought leaders can be found at the back of the book in the 'Resources Section'.*

Carl Jung's work on Shadow Self provides incredible insight into the various things that influence how we move through the world, and what we carry with us from our experiences, culture, and so much more.

Your shadow self contains all of the thoughts, beliefs, and experiences that you continue to carry with you. Jung shares that these experiences live in your shadow, a darkness that can elude you and influence your behavior.

When you check in with your body and become aware of what you are feeling, you shine a light into that darkness.

Your shadow self isn't necessarily bad, it's part of who you are and will always be with you. The negative aspect of the shadow lies in your unawareness. If you don't know what's following you through life, you never fully step into your greatest potential and the gifts you are here to share.

# The Power of Repetition!

This work is simple, but not easy. Many people put up road blocks in these early stages. They tell themselves they are too busy to pause and check in during their day. It's important to understand that these exercises are the building blocks needed to create the solid foundation that will support your hopes and dreams. The foundation that will support transformational change.

When you feel like you want to shut down to this work, go back to your initial list of why you started. How do you want to move through your day? Who do you want to be?

 Then take a deep breath and remember that all of this is truly accessible, you just have to keep showing up.

You are learning and remembering how to bring this awareness into your conscious behavior. You are in essence retraining yourself, and unraveling years of not paying attention. Make no mistake, these steps are important.

You are creating new habits, and forming habits takes time and commitment.

B.J. Fogg and James Clear both offer wonderful resources and support in the work of forming and breaking habits. You can find more information on both of their offerings in the 'Resources Section'.

Through their sharing, learn how you can make the process of creating habits of awareness fun and rewarding.

## Boundaries

Now is the perfect time to talk about boundaries. Boundaries within your own thoughts and awareness, and the boundaries you put in place with others.

In these early stages, you will create boundaries around your own thoughts and your interactions, some temporary and some permanent. This work requires you to be vulnerable. And learning to become vulnerable requires boundaries.

The reason it may be difficult to identify where you feel joy in your body is because that feeling exists within your most tender state. Within that vulnerability though lies your greatest power and your true soul center.

Believe it or not, you are learning to occupy a space within yourself where you will comfortably move through your day from that place of vulnerability. Why? Because it is in this state that you truly feel your connection and interconnection to all of life. It is in this state that your dreams are actualized, you find your purpose, and your true heart-centered wisdom.

Focus again on that memory that made you feel happy. Remember the feeling it gave you in the moment. Then, imagine moving through your day embodying that feeling of freedom and openness and having someone cut you down, discredit your ideas, or anything that would hurt.

When you are in these early stages of feeling vulnerable and happy in the same moment, those cut downs can knock you off your feet and send you right back into that "safe" place of not feeling — that "safe" place of ignoring, pushing through, and burying the feelings that leave you wide open and exposed.

As this work becomes second nature, your awareness and compassion become a layer of armor that allow you to stand fully in your true self and true work. You are no longer susceptible to the moods and whims of others. You know how to stand solidly on your path.

So during these early stages of reconnection with yourself, boundaries are crucial.

***Boundaries within your own thoughts***. Science has shown us that it takes ninety seconds for emotions to move through our bodies. Ninety seconds to feel and experience them, without analyzing them, in order for them to pass through us and not get lodged and create greater, prolonged turmoil.

So this first boundary is about setting the intention to give yourself the time and space you need to allow uncomfortable thoughts and events to move through you.

This boundary requires a commitment to pause, and notice what is taking place without analyzing, judging, or moving into your old stories. Look at your watch, count to ninety while breathing deeply, whatever it takes to put this boundary into action.

***Boundaries with others.*** As you step into this place of vulnerability, reconnection, and centering, boundaries with others are also of extreme importance. This work you are embarking on needs to be kept sacred until such a time when you can stand in your own vulnerability from a place of power and confidence.

This means only sharing this new awareness, these a-ha moments, with those you completely trust. Those you know can respect your boundaries and honor your process within this sacred space of discovery.

We sometimes expect this to include everyone that we love, and that isn't always the case. As you share this work with others, use your body to test if this person is a safe space right now. Pay attention to how you feel as you share, and how their response makes you feel.

**Boundaries within relationships.** You may need to verbalize certain boundaries as you move through the early stages of this work. (Remember these boundaries don't have to be permanent as you navigate these new waters.)

For example, when I first started down this road of reconnection with myself, I would notice times when I was in conversation with my husband and could feel myself move into that place of tension. In those moments, I learned to ask him for some time. I shared that I was feeling frustrated and unable to really hear him or share with him when I was feeling this way. This request for a boundary was always respected, and actually appreciated, as I learned to navigate this new world. Remember that this healing work truly does benefit all.

Let family members know that you are going to do some deep personal work and that you may need to pause during conversations, or take a little longer to make decisions.

They may not understand and that's okay. Your role isn't to bring everyone along on this journey with you. It's about creating the safe space you need for your own growth and awareness. Help them see, through your growth, that this is important to you, and will ultimately benefit you all.

## Relationships May Fall Away

You may notice that certain relationships begin to feel different. You begin to view them in a new light.

This awareness may mean that it's time for these relationships to shift, transition into their next phase, or come to an end. Some may naturally fall away, but so will old stories and beliefs.

As you evolve and learn more about yourself and the world around you, your relationships need to evolve as well.

This can be a natural adjustment that you enter into with those in your life in a powerful way by engaging in "restructuring" conversations from a place of joy and freedom in your body. These conversations can open up a new world of engagement and interaction with those around you when they are truly centered around, and coming from, your heart wisdom.

Anything that falls away during this time is, most likely, not serving you as you become more aligned with your true self. Trust it. Trust that this is best for everyone involved. Trust that beautiful people, opportunities, and abundance will come in a more holistic way that honors all involved.

The relationships that fall away are no longer serving *either* of you. This work you are doing is not only for you, but for those around you as well. Those in your immediate circle and in the larger global circle.

Expressing yourself authentically (from your true, heart-centered space of unconditional love) can rock the boat in your relationships. But this rocking is really bringing things back into alignment.

If a relationship orients around truth, it is truly orienting around love. Some relationships remain the same through this stage of growth and awareness, some may fall away, and others may shift within this new space and enter a new stage of connection.

Trust that all are transforming as they should when you engage from the place of joy and freedom within your body. All is aligning when you listen to, and are guided by, your heart.

Those who support you on this journey are meant to be part of your growth and greater work. That support can look like encouragement, inquiry, reflection, sharing, questioning, prodding, and so much more.

Don't discredit the difficult relationships either; they are also here to teach you lessons and keep you moving down your true path.

## Emotional Responsibility and Integrity

One of the components of this new awareness is recognizing the roles you've played in your old stories, relationships, and ventures.

As relationships, priorities, and dreams fall away, or shift (and this may not be part of your journey), it's important to take a look at the role you've played in the success and failure of those experiences, as well as experiences from your past.

Did you contribute to an emotional or relationship pattern that plays out again and again? Did you allow yourself to be treated in a way that wasn't true to your deeper needs and desires? Were you trying to achieve something, or hold onto something, that wasn't truly aligned with who you are working toward becoming? (Or truly, the person you already are, and are in the process of remembering.)

This is where your body becomes a powerful tool and gauge in your work. You can move into that place of heart-centered awareness within yourself, and ask if you are engaging from your highest sense of right and for the betterment of all involved. Your heart-centered wisdom that is accessed from that place of freedom and joy.

As you look back and visit some of your past experiences, it's important to notice the shift that needs to happen as relationships and situations change.

Powerful components of feminine wisdom are: expanded awareness and reflection, allowing, shifting, and acknowledging.

When you own your role within these experiences, you create space for a deeper level of love and greater alignment.

## Intuition vs Ego

This work you are doing is moving you toward complete heart-centered embodiment. You are learning to be present and tuned into your body as you move through your day.

So, how do you know when what you are feeling is deeper wisdom, and not simply your old stories showing up again?

How do you recognize when you are feeling that intuitive knowing? When the thoughts that come to you are coming from your feminine consciousness, your heart wisdom?

Your intuition comes from your heart. Moving the energy from your head to your heart is one of the key components of reconnecting with the feminine and changing how you lead in the world.

The following section on Heart Brain Coherence offers a powerful exercise for accessing the wisdom of your heart.

This is your next level of work. You have created a new awareness and conversation with yourself; now it's time to connect, or reconnect, with your deepest wisdom that comes from your heart.

Science has verified that we have three brains within our body: one in our gut, one in our heart, and one in our head. The brain that exists within your heart communicates more frequently to the brain within your head than the other way around. By disconnecting with the messages from your body, you have disconnected from this powerful wisdom.

It's time to reconnect and transform how you are guided through your days and interactions.

When you seek answers, you are either accessing that deeper intuitive knowing, or being influenced by your ego, old stories, learned behavior, and responses. Or another way to state it is this, you are either turning to the brain in your head or the brain in your heart.

Checking in with your body is an incredible gauge, and accessible tool, to discern whether what you are feeling is your intuition or your ego.

> "To be of ultimate service to the planet we must reconnect to that innate feminine knowing that comes from being rather than doing."
>
> ~ Sandra Ingerman

## Heart Brain Coherence

(You can find more information on the work of HeartMath and Gregg Braden in the 'Resources Section' of the book.)

HeartMath is an organization that has done powerful work around heart brain coherence, and the importance of connecting to the wisdom that's available to us at all times.

They share on their website, "As you bring your physical, mental and emotional systems into coherent alignment, you begin to experience increased access to your heart's intuitive guidance. Tuning into your heart's wisdom creates a profound shift within that helps you approach situations with more emotional balance, compassion, clarity, and personal confidence."

Gregg Braden has done a significant amount of work in this arena as well. He shares that: "the single eye of the heart is a state of harmony that we create for ourselves in heart-brain cohesion, accessing what's true for us in the moment of any given situation. Rather than thinking through a list of the pros and cons, or weighing out the probability that an experience of the past will repeat itself in the present, our heart knows instantly what's true for us right now."

I invite you to take a second, pause, and let that sharing land in your body. The opportunity in front of you right now is incredibly significant and life changing.

Braden offers powerful exercises on reconnecting with the wisdom of the heart. I use variations of his and HeartMath's exercises regularly as I move through decisions, think about opportunities, or dream into what is next.

This practice opens up a world of awareness that allows us to tap into the collective wisdom available to us at all times. It's a powerful guiding practice.

I'll walk you through a shortened version of the practice, and recommend you visit the resources shared by both HeartMath and Gregg Braden to move through their guided offerings as well.

Start by sitting in a comfortable position and relax. Don't try to control your breath, just notice it moving through your body.

From this relaxed state, place one or two fingers in the center of your chest and allow your awareness and attention to land in this point of connection.

Notice what you feel in your heart space as you bring your focus to this area. Hold the words compassion, joy, harmony in your thought and see if you can feel you heart responding.

I'm going to ask you a 'yes' and 'no' question. Silently repeat these questions to yourself and notice what happens in your body as you hold your awareness in your heart space.

First ask: **"My heart, am I reading a book by Laurie Benson?"** Notice how your heart responds.

Now ask: **"My heart, am I sitting on Mars?"** Again notice how your heart responds.

How our heart communicates, yes or no, will be different for us all. Some will feel sensations, others might see colors, or hear words. There is no right or wrong way.

If you felt a response, take a few moments and journal about what you felt.

Now see if you can move through this practice again, ask another question, and amplify that feeling coming from your heart. Using your focused awareness, and your breath, see if you can increase the sensation and energy. Become familiar with the responses, so they are easily recognizable as you move through your day.

**TIP:** Remember that all of these practices take time. If you didn't feel a response from your heart, you are not alone. As you move through your day, pay attention to questions where you already know the answer. Then, move through this exercise and ask your heart that question. Knowing the answer already, see if you can begin to notice anything. Pick easy questions to start and be kind to yourself.

For example, before you take a drink water, ask: **"My Heart, am I going to drink water?"** Then, notice.

You are creating a new relationship with your body, and every time you show up and check-in, things shift.

## Intuition vs Ego Exercise

This exercise takes you deeper into your heart wisdom. It allows you to discern whether you are moving forward influenced by old patterns, learned behaviors, and old stories, or whether are you being guided by your heart.

Your heart wisdom is connected to not only what is good and best for you, but also to what is good and best for all of life.

Our heart connects us to the collective consciousness. (See more resources from Gregg Braden and HeartMath on Global Coherence in the 'Resources Section'.)

**The Exercise:** Think about a question you are hoping to answer.

**Write down your question.**

Sit for a minute and listen to the answer that arises. **What is your immediate answer?**

Now turn your attention to your body. **What are you feeling right now?**

**Are you in a place of freedom and joy, or tension and anxiety?**

Wherever you are in your body, take a deep breath, and use the exhale to relax and release. Focus on allowing. Feel into your deeper knowing, your heart-centered wisdom.

Remember that you are searching for an answer that serves the greater good of you and everyone involved. Know that a deeper settling, and intention set in love, opens up access to your intuitive wisdom and knowing.

Now move through the Heart Cohesion exercise and ask your question to your heart, **"My heart…?"**

**Has anything changed?**

**Does it feel different than where you started?**

**Have you found a place of deeper clarity, or deeper peace?**

**Can you trust this feeling? Why or why not?**

## Stages of Consciousness

**Four Stages of Consciousness:** Micheal Beckwith has done incredible work in this arena of awareness and growth. He offers a masterclass on MindValley for those interested in taking a deeper dive.

**One caution:** Do not move into judgement of yourself or others because of where you show up in these stages. See the information shared here as an opportunity for further exploration and investigation.

The four stages of consciousness he discusses are:

**Victim Stage - To Us**
Victims feel the world is happening *to* them, and identify with their circumstances.

**Manifestor Stage - By Us**
Manifestors believe the world is happening *because* of their actions. Manifestors are goal oriented, and gain motivation from individuals or things. Manifestors begin living their best case scenarios, and their thinking and life experiences begin to change.

**Channel Stage - Through Us**
Channelers understand that the world is happening *through* them. Things are as they are meant to be. They understand their calling. They experience the unfolding of their soul because they are activating their potential. They act from their soul calling instead of how society wants them to be. This is the stage where life visioning begins. Channelers are vision oriented and receive inspiration from the divine.

**Being Stage - As Us**

In this final stage, we are connected to the flow of life. We move as one with all of existence.

These Four Stages of Consciousness offer great insight and frames of reference as you move through this work. They offer an opportunity to not only understand where you are in your own growth, but also provide insight and awareness of where others are on their journey. Notice without judgement.

As you become more centered in your own awareness, it is easier to recognize when someone is operating from within the Victim Stage, or when you are. This recognition creates an opportunity to not hold, or own, the experience. Practice letting it move through you without getting stuck.

This awareness allows you to witness interactions in a new way. No longer taking the actions of others personally, but instead seeing them where they currently are and recognizing the opportunity and potential for their growth and greater awareness.

It also opens the door to the powerful question, "Is this experience or feeling mine to hold?"

We are often impacted by the feelings, moods, and experiences of others. We can again use our hearts as beautiful guides and ask if what we are feeling before, after, and during interactions is truly ours. This is ultimately what you are moving toward, occupying your heart-centered wisdom in all experiences.

This question can be informative and incredibly freeing. If the answer is no, you know to let it go and move on. If the answer is yes, then you have gained important awareness into an area of your beliefs, and a way you are moving through the world. The invitation is to then unpack and let go of it in its own time.

Awareness is the first step in change.

When you see this opportunity for growth and greater awareness in yourself and others, the role you play in your interactions shifts.

You no longer need to react from a place that defends your way of being or thinking. You no longer feel that the actions of others are directed at you, even if they believe they are.

You understand that each interaction is an opportunity for growth and greater awareness for all involved. You open the door to support others in a new way, one truly coming from your heart-based soul center.

# Section 3: The Rubber Hits the Road

## Your True Work

In *Return of the Feminine and the World Soul*, Llewellyn Vaughan-Lee explains that when we heal ourselves, we free up the energy of the planet to do the healing work she needs to do as well. Heal Yourself - Heal the World.

I know that feels like a huge stretch, but there is incredible truth behind that strong statement.

When you heal the areas of your awareness that have been holding you back, the ways in which you have been standing in your own way, you create the opportunities for others around you to do the same.

Energy flows where attention goes. When you can move through the world from your heart-centered, embodied, power, you no longer need to focus all of your attention and energy on yourself.

You are good. You are confident. You are whole, complete, and no longer looking for experiences to fill a void within you. You know the work you are here to do. It is from this embodied and fully aware space that you step into your greatest work. You are no longer looking for situations to feed your ego; you are a living example of what it means to be in-service to the greater good. Your freedom is opening up access to the healing and shift for others as well.

That freedom allows you to notice the greater needs of those around you — the people, the planet, and all living things. By putting your attention on other beings (once you are whole and complete yourself), you create the powerful opportunity to see your interconnection.

You understand that the actions of others aren't meant to hurt you, but are a reflection of the pain, or joy, they are feeling. You begin to witness their pain and view their actions from a place of compassion. You don't condone or condemn their actions, instead you are able to allow them the space they need to continue on their own healing journey.

This is your greatest work in life.

This is all of our greatest work in life.

When you notice, and feel, and truly see, then your role, and the actions you need to take, become clear. Your true path and power is evident.

This will look different for us all. We each have our own unique gifts to share. From this new state of clarity and awareness, we bring our individual experience and wisdom necessary to create collective change.

I want you to take a moment and go back to your original list of why you stepped into this work.

**How does this list feel now?**

**Has anything shifted?**

**Do you feel the path forward?**

**Is there anything that you would like to add now?**

**Are you excited about the opportunity in front of you?**

Then go back to the list of Feminine Leadership Qualities.

**Have these shifted or expanded for you?**

**If so, how?**

**What do you want to add or take away?**

Now sit with this sharing: The work you have done, and will continue to do, will create the global shift the world needs.

That is a big statement and can easily send us back into our old stories, or the stories handed to us by everything created under the Eagle paradigm.

This doesn't mean that our "work" has to be some ground-breaking discovery, or have a huge mission. Our most important work is this reconnection with ourselves, each other, and all of life. The work right here in front of us.

Sit quietly for a moment, connect with your heart, and then feel what happens when you read this statement: By moving through the world from this heart-centered space of awareness and action, you are connected to the greater good of all of life, and holding the space needed for transformative change.

What could be more monumental than that?!

**How did your heart respond?**

**Do you believe it?**

**Can you trust it as the truth?**

## Exercise

Take a moment to pause and feel everything that was just shared. Give yourself the time to breathe it in. Notice what is moving through you.

If I were to ask you right now what you are here to do, what would you share? Don't second guess yourself, or let the negative, or what we often deem "rational" thoughts come in. What do you intuitively feel in this moment?

**What are you here to do?**

**Does this feel true to you?**

**Are you able to trust this answer? Why or why not?**

Make a commitment to yourself to stay centered. Move through your days as the best possible version of yourself, and notice how this allows you to experience the world in a new way.

When you occupy this intuitive space of allowing and deeper knowing, what do you notice about those around you? How have your experiences changed?

What is welling up in you that wants to move into action? What wants to manifest as next steps on your personal journey? Or do you simply need to pause and find stillness at this time?

**Take a moment to write down your thoughts.**

## The Elements of Feminine Leadership
## This is Our Time

> "It's also important to remember that the
> divine feminine is not in any contrast or
> opposition to the masculine. Within her sacred
> wholeness everything is included."
>
> ~ Llewellyn Vaughan-Lee

It's time to stop over analyzing, second guessing, judging, and even trying to make sense of this new knowledge and awareness that is presenting itself to so many of us right now.

We haven't ever been here before. We have no frame of reference to turn to for guidance. Instead, our guidance is showing up in ways we've never experienced.

We are learning in meditation and prayer, recalling memories, and receiving messages from our ancestors. We are literally downloading information and instructions from spirit guides that leave us questioning all that we have been told is true.

Some of us are simply aware that there is a collective power at play, our collective consciousness and awareness is creating this drive, this urgency, to step into something bigger. Bigger not in the sense of massive projects, etc. (although those are alright too) but bigger in the sense of shifting the trajectory of humanity and the planet by reconnecting with, and being guided by, our heart wisdom.

If we feel into our bodies, we understand that this awareness isn't just about us. There is something deeper, older, ancestral that feels like an emergence from within.

So many of us are holding this "new" ancient wisdom close to our chests. Feeling like we should share it with someone, but recognizing the potential ridicule we will open ourselves up to when we put these stories and messages out there for all to see. Remember that this wisdom has been silenced for many generations from within the Eagle paradigm. Our current structures and systems haven't supported the voice of the feminine. We are creating new languages and ways of expressing what is moving through us at our deepest level of awareness and consciousness.

Let me be clear, this is the work of the divine feminine, and the time to share is now.

We must learn to communicate from a place that is vulnerable and free, recognizing that our power resides within this place of vulnerability and centered awareness. We must first see ourselves before we can truly see others, and see the changes needed in the world.

We aren't alone in this large quest, and that knowing can bring us incredible freedom. We have an army of support showing up in ways that are new and unfamiliar. This support is coming to us in our dreams, in the form of new and emerging ideas, from the younger generations who challenge how we communicate and view one another, and from our deeper intuitive knowing. We can either openly embrace this support, or continue to stand alone and watch things escalate and spin out of control.

If there truly is only one path forward, and it's the one we are currently on, our fate is pretty clear. But, you know and feel what is true. You sense the powerful opportunity in front of us all right now.

The choice really is ours. It takes setting aside the ego, and letting go of the belief that what we've been taught in our schools, religions, anything established under the masculine Eagle paradigm, is the only way.

Everything we are experiencing today from climate change to war are manifestations of our deep disconnection; our disconnection from our intuitive, feminine voice.

Sit with that for a moment. If there really is only one way, and it's the path we've been on up until now, then we truly are doomed. But if you sit in nature, and watch the wind play with the trees, allowing your focus to land on your breath, and just feel, is there a twinge of something else? Something more stirring in you? A connection or familiarity that you want to understand on a deeper level?

What if I told you that the water you drink, the water that flows through you, is the same water that flowed through the dinosaurs? It is the same water that will flow through whatever and whoever next stands on Mother Earth. Can you feel that sharing stir something deep within you?

Does this awareness allow you to shift out of the "power over" paradigm we have lived within for far too long? The paradigm that views all of life as expendable, and works to eliminate the awareness of our interconnection? Is there a deeper wisdom that moves through you? Maybe even one you can't quite yet hold? Like a word resting right on the tip of your tongue? Feel into your body.

What if it could be that simple? What if a twinge of awareness is where the change begins? On a global level, what if we begin to accept and believe in life and consciousness outside of our teachings and current knowing? That global awareness could open the door to the incredible shifts that are needed and possible.

This is the beautiful gift of the work you are doing. It's a tool, a gauge, a resource accessible and waiting to offer guidance and insight at all times.

It means allowing instead of pushing, trusting in the unknown, and having the courage to be the voice that stands up and shares this new way of thinking and being. You have the tools now to be a player in this necessary change.

I know that the courageous ones, the voices stepping out, are the ones bringing the armies we need. You belong among them. They are the ones opening the doors for us to truly see and understand what is happening. You can now show us how to move *with* these shifts, instead of *against* them. You truly can, and we need to learn through your words, experiences, and teachings.

You are the voice of the divine feminine. This wisdom is being shared through both men and women, and the time is critically, now.

This wisdom is yours to share. And this deep work is the path to the collective deeper knowing and your heart-centered true voice.

> "We are present at a time when the world is dying and waiting to be reborn, and all the words in our libraries and on the Internet will not tell us what to do. But the sacred feminine can share with us her secrets, tell us how to be, how to midwife her rebirth. And because we are her children, she can speak to each of us, if we have the humility to listen."
>
> ~ Llewellyn Vaughan-Lee

This awareness work takes time, practice, and commitment. Meeting these new feelings with curiosity and kindness is definitely crucial until you reach the point where they become second nature.

I can now, in the moment, recognize where I am in my body and pause because I've been practicing, and will continue to practice, this work of awareness and embodiment. I now know that this tool of embodiment, enabling myself to be completely present in the moment, is a critical and necessary step in awakening to my true self, and returning to a place of balance.

It is the next step in moving through the world guided by the interconnected feminine wisdom needing to resurface.

# Embodiment

Now that you have moved through the somatic awareness work, and can connect with the wisdom being shared from your heart, I want to offer another tool for feeling into what's moving through your body, hoping for your attention.

This has proven to be a powerful healing tool on my journey, and I hope it will be on yours as well.

Many of us have been taught in mediation, and our quieter practices, the power and goal of disconnecting from our bodies. I've found that this desired end goal actually pulls me further away from my feminine wisdom.

Feminine wisdom is accessible through embodiment. When you feel the breath moving through your body, feel the energy rising up through the earth and along your spine, you are interconnected to all of life.

The feminine is accessed through your ability to fully reside in, and embody, the current moment.

Embodying the moment means being present in life as it is, instead of how you want it to be.

Feminine wisdom and consciousness exist together in this complete embodiment. This awareness brings quite a few of our trainings and practices into question.

Let's remember that we are all moving into a time of newness and unknown. A time to question what feels off, pay attention to the areas of our life that have felt difficult and out of alignment. What practices in your life do you feel called to visit and perhaps shift?

A strong example of this new inquiry for me has been around meditation. I've learned over the years that meditation done properly brings a quiet presence, allowing me to disconnect from my thoughts and enter another realm of awareness.

This form of meditation has served me well, and also continued to be a challenge. Thinking about how my feminine wisdom resides in my ability to maintain complete embodiment and presence, has caused me to explore a new form of meditation.

I'm calling this experiment, Embodiment Meditation. This is a living experiment, so I've done my best to describe my experience, and the process to date.

# Embodiment Meditation

In this practice, I quiet my thoughts, and focus completely on the energy moving through my body.

What's tingling, pulsing, where is the energy strongest in this moment? Instead of moving out of my body, I stay present within it, present in the energy that is showing up.

I've learned that cultivating this practice of staying present in my body, while quieting my thoughts, is bringing to the surface my true intuitive awareness.

As I follow the energy within my body, it begins to highlight and accentuate the areas that may need extra attention and release.

(This practice has also been deeply influenced by the study of Epigenetics, recognizing that dis-ease is actually stored energy that needs our attention, in order for us to release it and let it go. I highly recommend you take a look at the teachings of Bruce Lipton and the work he has done on Epigenetics to understand how energy is stored in our bodies and the healing power of letting it move through us. You can find more in the 'Resources Section'.)

**Here are the steps I'm using for this practice:**

Sit in a comfortable position with your hands resting on your knees, palms facing up.

Close your eyes and take a few relaxing breaths. Don't try to control your breath, simply use it to relax into your body.

Bring your attention to the palms of your hands. Notice the tingling and pulsing present at their center, and let your attention rest there.

(If you need to activate this energy, use the forefinger of one hand and make small, gentle circles in the center of your other palm. Now change hands, do the same, and let them land palms up on our lap. Let your complete awareness fall in the center of your hands. Imagine your breath moving into your palms and feel the energy increase as you hold your focus there.)

When you are fully present with this feeling, allow your attention to move deeper into your body. Using your breath, imagine the energy in your hands moving up your arms and into your core.

Without analyzing what you are feeling, or why these feelings are present, notice what other areas are wanting your attention. Where is the energy showing up? You may feel it as tense, fluttery, zingy, there is no right or wrong feeling.

Using your breath as your tool, stay present in the area of your body asking for the attention.

As you breathe into this area, focus on releasing and letting go. Allow the energy to shift, move, and find its exit point. Visualize this release happening. (You may feel an immediate release, or it may take time and continued attention.)

Listen to your body, and what it's asking of you. You may feel like moving or exhaling with an open mouth, honor these requests. Without giving too much thought to these impulses, simply allow your body to show you what it needs, and then, move into this action in a way that is natural and free.

This new (for me) form of meditation has been easier than any I've explored in the past. I walk away from this practice feeling a sense of peace and centering that I haven't been able to achieve through meditation before.

I can only attribute this new experience to the fact that this practice honors my intuitive knowing. I'm allowing myself to access my feminine consciousness in a way that is true to this deeper wisdom and power.

# New Baseline

So what does all of this mean in terms of leadership and shifting how you move through your days? So much. This new layer of awareness becomes your baseline for engagement, conversation, and greater life planning.

You learn to check in as you move through the day and recognize the space you are occupying in your body. If you are in that space of freedom and joy, then you can have those big conversations, make harder decisions, and engage with your family and friends in a way that is most aligned with who you are. You show up as your best self.

When you are in that space of your old stories, anxiety, doubt, then you move through the day with more caution. You recognize the role you will play in every interaction when you engage from this place. You tip-toe through your responsibilities until you can shift and release whatever has put you in this space within yourself.

As this becomes second nature, your world truly opens in ways you never could have imagined. Things no longer happen *to* you. Instead you become a witness to the experiences of others, as well as your own. You allow these experiences to interplay with yours, but not control yours.

You understand, and feel, that the comments that used to offend were never really meant for you. The actions of others are just their stories playing out in real time.

As you become more centered in your truth and power, you create the opportunity for others to step into theirs as well.

When you shift the way you engage with, and witness the world around you, when you begin to see and understand things from your heart-centered wisdom, you create paradigm shifts. Old beliefs about yourself and others fall away. You feel your connection, interconnection, and responsibility. You embody all that you truly are, opening up this powerful opportunity for others.

So when I say this work is simple, but not easy, I truly mean it. Your greatest work is recognizing and owning how you embody your power, emotions, and beliefs. With great awareness, comes great responsibility.

If you are to be true to yourself, and those around you, you can no longer ignore what you understand. Once you learn the power of embodiment and accessing your heart wisdom, you up the game.

You will be able to tell when you are out of integrity, when a bad conversation was in great part due to what you were feeling in your body. And also when you should pause and shift within yourself before continuing, instead of pushing through.

This is how you lead from the feminine. This is feminine wisdom. Allowing instead of pushing. Allowing what you are feeling to move through you so you can come back to your thoughts, conversations, and interactions when you are truly in a space that allows for freedom and growth.

You move forward with the actions that are truly moving toward connection and unity.

This work allows others to receive your gifts, hear your words of wisdom, and share in your greater dreams.

## Redefining Value and Success
## Creating a New Language

The definitions of success, and how you value yourself, have been largely defined under the masculine Eagle paradigm. The words that have guided your actions, reactions, and interactions no longer serve the space you occupy now.

Close your eyes and visualize a successful person. What does their life look like?

For many of us, these images include wealth, power, and drive. These aren't bad qualities when they remain in balance, but we come up against strong feelings of self-worth and achievement when we are called to do work in the world that isn't rewarded in this same way.

This is where you step into redefining and re-evaluating what is truly important to you.

Merriam-Webster Dictionary defines success as a "favorable or desired outcome". This description still holds true on the path we are currently exploring. We are challenged when we add on the cultural and societal expectations that have expanded that definition.

If success is the manifestation of your greatest dreams and wishes coming to fruition, what does this look like? How do you redefine what this word means and how it makes you feel?

Take a moment to move through the magic wand exercise that follows.

## Magic Wand Exercise

If you could wave a magic wand, what would your life look like? Take the time to include everything and anything — travel, peaceful, exciting, healthy relationships, strong community, abundance, whatever comes to mind.

**Make your list.**

Now settle into your body. What do you *feel* as you read your list? If these are the things you truly want from life, what does success *feel* like for you?

**Write down your definition of success based on what you just experienced.** Focus on how it makes you feel.

When you focus on how success feels for you, does it shift your ability to see yourself as "successful"?

Let's consider this new definition of success as your working goal. The next word that comes up for many of us is value.

Can you value yourself and your work if the success you achieve doesn't look like the success of others around you?

Can you value yourself when others don't see you fitting into the cultural and traditional definition of success?

The answer of course is yes, *and* it takes work. This is again where the embodiment work comes into play. Every time you question whether your contribution is valuable, or question your own personal value, turn your attention inward.

Take a deep breath and settle in. As you exhale, let everything go. Then ask yourself this:

**Do I truly believe that my work is lacking value?**

**Do I truly believe that I lack value?**

I would hope that these questions land in your body with a resounding NO! It might mean that you have to refocus your attention to how these questions make you *feel*, and not the thoughts and judgments racing around in your head as you read them.

How does your heart answer these questions? And can you trust the answer coming from your heart, and not the programmed, conditioned answer coming from your head?

This realignment and redefinition is a critical piece of stepping into the feminine. You have to set the example and the bar of achievement and success at a new level. A level that celebrates the gifts and work that are desperately needed in the world, the ones that come from your heart wisdom.

This is a great time to again visit the list of Feminine Leadership Qualities. Who do you want to be?

## Allowing vs Pushing

This is one of my greatest areas of focus and personal work. I regularly get caught up in the cycle of wanting to do something bigger, now. I feel an urgency to do big work in the world. And because of this need, this is where I am most frequently challenged.

My story goes something like this… I've done the prep work, and I'm ready. So why do I have to wait? And what am I supposed to be *doing* right now while I wait?

When these questions arise, I have to sit and settle into my body again. I have to reconnect with the wisdom coming from my heart and allow the answers to find me in a new way.

Allowing takes time, patience, and vulnerability. We must release how we think things should look, and recognize and accept that the next steps are already in play. We are learning to accept divine timing instead of our own desired timeline.

When I let go of the need to make things happen, I recognize and remember that this "waiting period" is actually part of the work. I'm not waiting to get started, I'm in it.

This dissolving of old beliefs and ways of moving through the world is a big part of stepping into your heart wisdom and operating under a feminine paradigm.

This is the time of the Condor Rising, and this emerging way of leading from the feminine is bringing us back into a balanced state of unity and connection.

The change begins with us, and the work you have done has made you ready to face this greater challenge, or invitation. It's time to let go of human will and invite what's next to move into place.

This doesn't mean letting go of your drive and commitment, or the passion that gets you out of bed every morning. It means coming back to the practice of embodiment, being completely present in the moment, and accessing your heart wisdom, so that your engagement around your drive, commitment, and passion is truly aligned with your greatest power and purpose.

When you push toward something, you move out of the now, and often, switch from your heart to your head. You move into the Eagle paradigm, operating within the techniques and tendencies that you've been taught for most of your life. This is your natural default mode. It's all most of us have known up until now.

Becoming present in the now, practicing embodiment, *feeling* what you want to accomplish, and focusing your attention on the opportunities being presented to you, is the allowing verses the pushing.

It is in this space that you open yourself up to your greatest work and create global change.

**Some Questions to Ponder:**

**How can working with the feminine empower you to meet the call of our present time from a new perspective?**

**Can you draw on the wisdom of interconnectedness, embodiment, and reverence for all life when you think about what you're stepping into?**

**How can you listen for what you don't yet know?**

**What new awareness have you acquired that allows you to listen in a new way?**

**What does it mean to reclaim the feminine? In your life? In leadership?**

## Leading From the Feminine

The beauty of all of this work is that you are helping to define what it means to truly lead from the feminine at this moment in time.

There isn't a prescription for what it needs to look like in action, or even the significant change it will bring. This I do know though, it has to happen, and we are the ones bringing it forward.

The world needs us to understand and recognize the opportunity in front of us; an opportunity to step into our heart-based wisdom, and chart a new path.

The old ways are no longer working, so what option do we truly have other than stepping in and giving it our all.

Humanity and the planet deserve an opportunity to exist in a time and place guided by our deep, feminine truth, a time and place rediscovered within our interconnected hearts.

By stepping into this work, you are pioneering the rebirth of feminine wisdom. Bringing it back into the collective consciousness, back into conversation, and back into heart-based action.

I am honored to be on this journey with you and have so much hope for the future and the world we are calling forth through this powerful work and awareness.

# Resources

**Llewellyn Vaughan-Lee**
Book: Return of the Feminine and the World Soul
Website: Working with Oneness
https://workingwithoneness.org

**Carl Jung, Shadow Self**
Book: The Collected Works of C.G. Jung, Volume 7 in his essay The Relations Between the Ego and the Unconscious
Website: https://www.carl-jung.net/shadow.html

**Tara Brach**
Website: https://www.tarabrach.com to access her online meditations, talks, and teachings.

**James Clear**
Book: Atomic Habits

**B.J. Fogg**
Book: TinyHabits
Website: https://tinyhabits.com

**HeartMath**
Website: https://www.heartmath.com
Global Coherence: https://www.heartmath.org/gci/

**Gregg Braden**
Book: Human by Design
Book: Resilience from the Heart
Website: https://www.greggbraden.com

**4 Stages of Consciousness, Michael Beckwith**
Audio: Life Visioning: A Four-Stage Evolutionary Journey
to Live as Divine Love found on Amazon
Mindvalley Course: Michael Beckwith's Life Visioning
Course: https://www.mindvalley.com/visioning

**Bruce Lipton, Epigenetics**
Book: The Biology of Belief
Website: https://www.brucelipton.com

**Online Community for Women: https://
www.inwardboundcommunity.com**

# Staying in Touch

I would love to hear about your continued journey into embodying the feminine, and all of the other goodness that comes from this deep and powerful work.

The gifts you bring are amazing and so needed. I cannot wait to see your unique way of Leading From the Feminine!

Please consider joining myself, and other incredible women, in our online community where we explore these topics, move through practices, and so much more.

www.lnwardBoundCommunity.com